W0037785

Thanks to Don Moore,
Director of the Oregon Zoo,
for his careful review of this book.

Copyright © 2020 Clavis Publishing Inc., New York

Originally published as *Superbeesjes. Bouwers* in Belgium and the Netherlands by Clavis Uitgeverij, 2019
English translation from the Dutch by Clavis Publishing Inc., New York

Visit us on the Web at www.clavis-publishing.com.

No part of this publication may be reproduced or stored in a retrieval system, or transmitted in any form or by any means,
electronic, mechanical, photocopying, recording, or otherwise, without the prior written permission of the publisher,
except in the case of brief quotations embodied in critical articles and reviews.
For information regarding permissions, write to Clavis Publishing, info-US@clavisbooks.com.

Super Animals: Builders written by Reina Ollivier and Karel Claes,
and illustrated by Steffie Padmos

ISBN 978-1-60537-578-6

This book was printed in May 2020 at Neografia, a.s.,
Sučianska 39A, 038 61 Martin-Priekopa, Slovakia.

First Edition
10 9 8 7 6 5 4 3 2 1

Clavis Publishing supports the First Amendment
and celebrates the right to read.

SUPER ANIMALS

BUILDERS

Written by **Reina Ollivier** & **Karel Claes**
Illustrated by **Steffie Padmos**

Clavis
NEW YORK

Just like people, animals need a place to live. The animals in this book build their homes. Sometimes it's high in a tree, and sometimes it's hidden under the ground. They use earth, branches, and leaves or whatever they can find nearby.
Each house has its own style, from small and simple to large and complex.
There are animals that prefer to live alone and others that live in groups.
Animals build nests, dig tunnels, build roads and dams and webs.
Come and discover who these special builders are!

CONTENTS

BEAVER

I have a big family. Sometimes there are eight of us living together. That's why we build big houses by the water, called lodges.

9

Who am I?

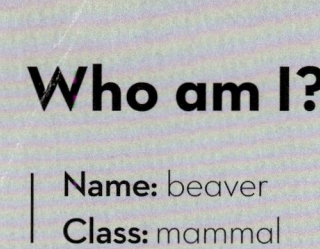

Name: beaver
Class: mammal

Builds with teeth and paws

Size: 27–40 inches (70–100 centimeters) (minus tail); males and females are the same size

Legs:
2 short front legs
2 wide hind legs

Teeth that **keep growing,** but never get too long because of all the gnawing

Paws:
front paws are used like we use our hands; hind paws have webbing between the toes to help with swimming

Double nail
on the second toe

Wide, flat tail
with scales

Habitat:
near streams, rivers, ponds, lakes, and swamps

Food:
leaves, bark, twigs, roots, and plants

Swimming speed:

0   5 mph   100

Enemies:

 fox  wolf  bear  wild boar  wild cat  puma  lynx  wolverine

I sleep much of the day.
I am most active in **the evening** and **at night.**

When there is **danger, I hit** the water **hard with my tail.**

I am **slow on land,** but **faster in the water.** I can swim underwater for 15 minutes without coming up for air.

I use the **double nail** on my hind foot to comb mud and dirt from my fur.

My lips close behind my big front teeth. This way I can **gnaw underwater** without getting water in my mouth. And my ears, eyes, and nose are designed to keep water out.

I leave a **scent** where I live, so other beavers know that this is my home. And believe it or not, it smells pretty good. Some people say my scent smells like vanilla.

This is our lodge, made of tree trunks, branches, and mud. Ours has two entrances underwater. Some lodges have only one. Inside there are one or two rooms. The first we use to shake our fur dry. We live together in the other room. Both rooms are above the surface of the water and stay dry.

The thick walls of our lodge, and the underwater entrances, keep predators out. When our lodge is in shallow water, we build a dam. The dam helps water levels rise.

CROSS SPIDER

Every day I weave a large web using sticky spider threads. I use the web to collect my food. When an insect flies in, my web might get a hole in it, so I fix it. Then the next day I start all over again, making a new web.

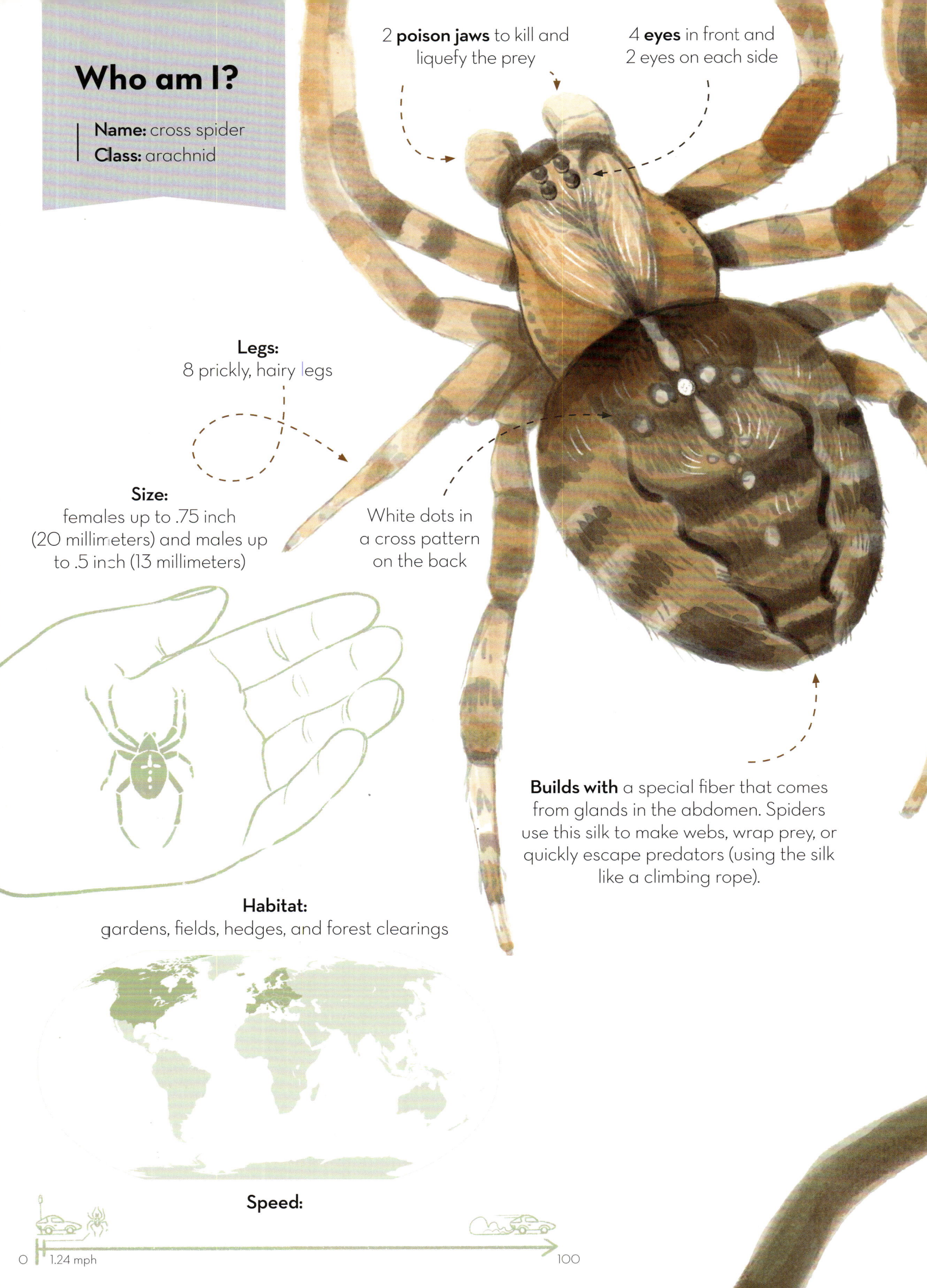

Who am I?

Name: cross spider
Class: arachnid

2 poison jaws to kill and liquefy the prey

4 eyes in front and 2 eyes on each side

Legs:
8 prickly, hairy legs

Size:
females up to .75 inch (20 millimeters) and males up to .5 inch (13 millimeters)

White dots in a cross pattern on the back

Builds with a special fiber that comes from glands in the abdomen. Spiders use this silk to make webs, wrap prey, or quickly escape predators (using the silk like a climbing rope).

Habitat:
gardens, fields, hedges, and forest clearings

Speed:

O | 1.24 mph   100

Food:
flying insects

Enemies:
mainly birds

I don't have a skeleton. Inside, everything is soft.
To **grow** I **molt,** kind of like a snake. When my skin falls off,
I grow very fast until my new skin is hard.

All **spiders** bite, but only a few spiders are **dangerous.**
Not me. Spiders bite when they are scared. My bite hurts
because of the **poison** I inject, but it's such a small
amount that it won't harm you.

I am **not an insect,** because insects only have six legs.
I'm an arachnid, as are scorpions, ticks, and mites.

When I move, I mostly have
four legs in the air and **four on
the ground.** I also use my front
legs to explore my surroundings.
I have **eight eyes,** but I can't
see very far.

If you **bother** me, I'll **shake my web** to scare you off.
If that doesn't help, I'll drop a thread from
my web and run away.

17

This is the web I've just woven. It's still very
sticky, so it's great for catching insects.
I also weave a few threads that don't stick,
so I can walk on them. When there is a lot
of dust in my web, it becomes less sticky.
I can use these threads like a balloon.
They are lifted by the wind and can take
me to another place. A fun way to travel!

I like to build my web in a sunny place, where there's not too much wind. First, I make support points. Then, I weave from the middle to the outer edges and around. It looks a bit like the spokes of a bicycle wheel, don't you think? Tthat's why some people call it a wheel web. My web can be up to 16 inches (40 centimeters) in size.

With my head down, I wait for an insect to get stuck in my web. Sometimes I wrap my prey in silk and save it for later.

SOCIABLE WEAVER

I like company. We live with many other families in a huge nest. Grandmas and grandpas, parents and children, all take care of each other. I help find food for the young birds.

Who am I?

Name: sociable weaver
Class: bird

We find most of our **food** on the ground, but also on tree trunks and **leaves**. We love **termites**. We usually search for food in **groups**.

Size:
5.5 inches
(14 centimeters); males
and females are the
same size

Legs:
2

My **appearance** may remind you of a **house sparrow**. My **beak** is **firmer** and has a **blue-gray** color.

Builds with
beak and feet

Habitat:
in tropical grassland with
a few tall trees

Food:
mainly insects,
but also seeds
and fruits

Speed:

30 mph   100

We are very **hospitable** and make our nest available to other birds. Finches, lovebirds, and African pygmy falcons like to live with us.

Our **nests** are very big, up to **10 feet** (3 meters) high and **20 feet** (6 meters) long. Sometimes as many as **five hundred** birds live there, all year round. You might compare it to an apartment building full of families.

But nests can become so heavy that the trees they are built in collapse.

Nests can last for a long time. There are nests that are more than a **hundred years old.**

Enemies:

snakes   monkeys   rats

Females lay an average of **3 eggs** at a time at least **four times a year.** This is important because more than half of the young birds are eaten by snakes. But if we stay alive, we can live a long time. Sociable weavers can live up to **ten years,** which is a long time for a bird.

23

Don't you think our nest looks impressive? It may look like a hay-stack, but it's very strong. We make the sloping roof with twigs. For the inside we use grass. We cover the nesting rooms with soft material, such as hair and feathers.

Nesting rooms are deep inside, and they stay warm. We sleep there at night when the temperature outside drops. We use the rooms closer to the wall to stay cool during the heat of the day.

If you look at the bottom, you'll see dozens of entrances. They lead to tunnels that take us to rooms inside.

We usually build our nests in trees with a long trunk and high branches. But a utility pole can also be an excellent option. Since the pole is slippery, intruders cannot reach our nest.

25

TERMITE

I live in a big hill that I helped build with a few million others. I work hard. You see me here with my queen. All she has to do is eat and lay eggs. I have a busy life with a lot of jobs. Building is one of my jobs.

Who am I?

Name: termite

Class: insect

Two antennae and strong **jaws** to chew wood

Size:
workers .1–.75 inch
(0.3–2 centimeters);
queen 2–4 inches
(5–10 centimeters)

Legs:
6

Food:
mainly wood, but also
dead leaves and waste

Termites don't make
a **sound;** they talk to one
another through **smell.**

We look like ants, but we're
not in the same family as ants.
We are related to **cockroaches.**

Habitat:
warm, tropical areas

Every termite has its own **job** in our
termite hill. **Workers** like me **build** the
nest, take **care** of the **queen** and the
eggs, and bring food. **Soldiers** guard
the entrances. They have **sharp jaws,**
which they use to spray poison.

All **workers** are **white** because our
bodies never see the sun. The soldiers
are **light brown** in color since they
come out during the day.

Speed:

0   1.24 mph

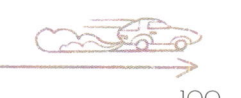

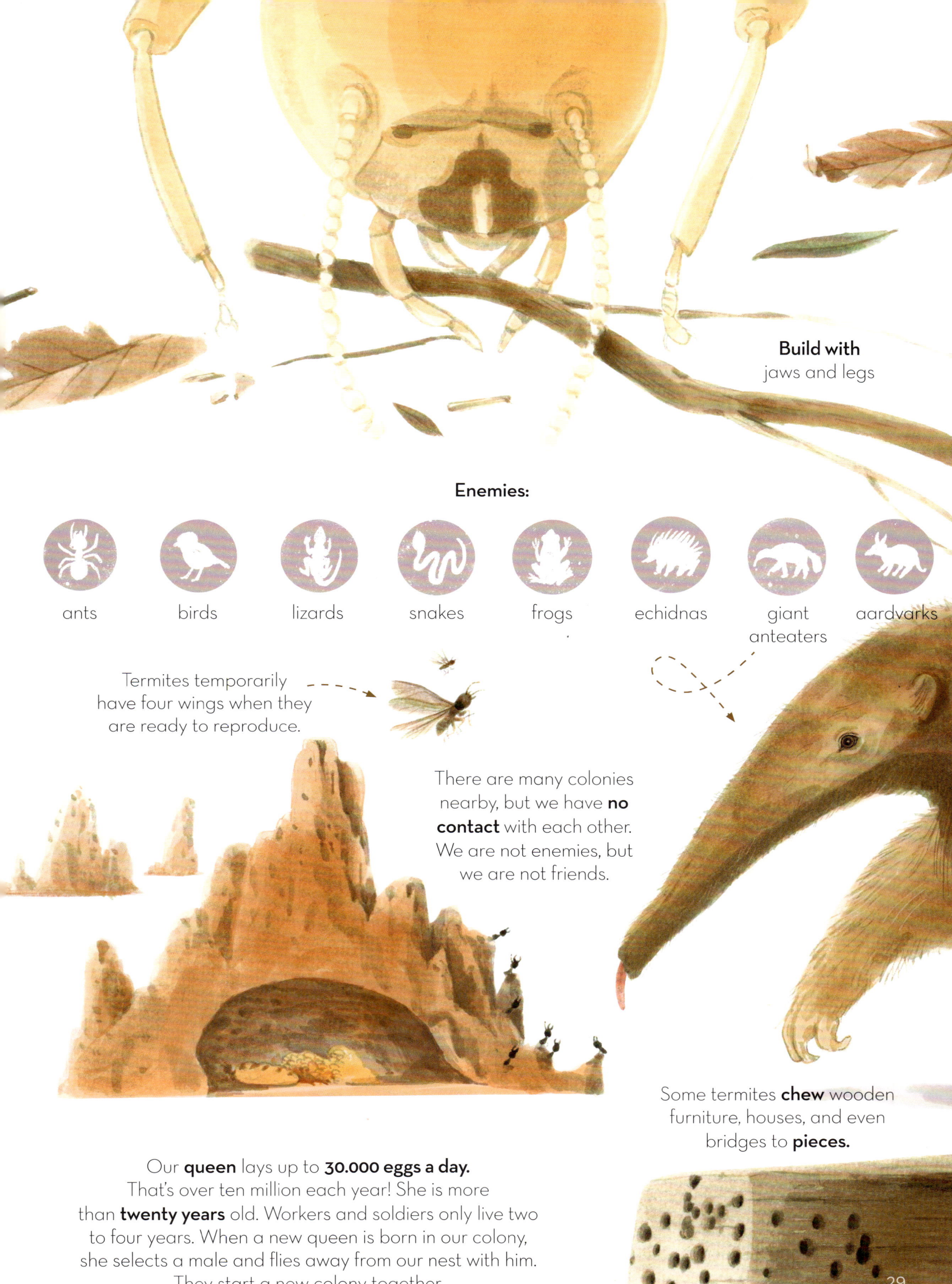

Build with
jaws and legs

Enemies:

| ants | birds | lizards | snakes | frogs | echidnas | giant anteaters | aardvarks |

Termites temporarily have four wings when they are ready to reproduce.

There are many colonies nearby, but we have **no contact** with each other. We are not enemies, but we are not friends.

Some termites **chew** wooden furniture, houses, and even bridges to **pieces.**

Our **queen** lays up to **30.000 eggs a day.** That's over ten million each year! She is more than **twenty years** old. Workers and soldiers only live two to four years. When a new queen is born in our colony, she selects a male and flies away from our nest with him. They start a new colony together.

29

Our termite hills can be up to 32 feet (10 meters) high. We use sand, chewed wood, and dung, which we glue together with saliva.
Our structure is so strong that you would need a heavy hammer to break the wall.

At the top we leave a small opening. This is a chimney where heat can escape, because we live in areas where it gets very hot. We build tunnels in the sidewalls to bring in fresh air.

Underneath the breeding room, where the queen stays, we make a network of tunnels where we bring the eggs and food. We don't have bedrooms, because we never sleep.

STORK

Do you recognize me by my long red beak? I build my nest high up in a tree, on a tower, or on the chimney of a house. From there I have a beautiful view. In autumn it gets too cold for me here, and I fly south. In spring I return to my nest in the north.

Who am I?

Name: stork
Class: bird

Builds with
beak and legs

Doesn't **sing** like other birds,
but **rattles** with the beak

Size:
about 3 feet (1 meter) high;
males are slightly larger
than females

Legs:
2 long legs

Wingspan of about
6 feet (2 meters)

Habitat:
in open areas with tall trees,
wet grasslands, swamps

Food:
mainly insects, snails, and earthworms;
also mice, frogs, moles, lizards and snakes

Speed:

0

40.5 mph

100

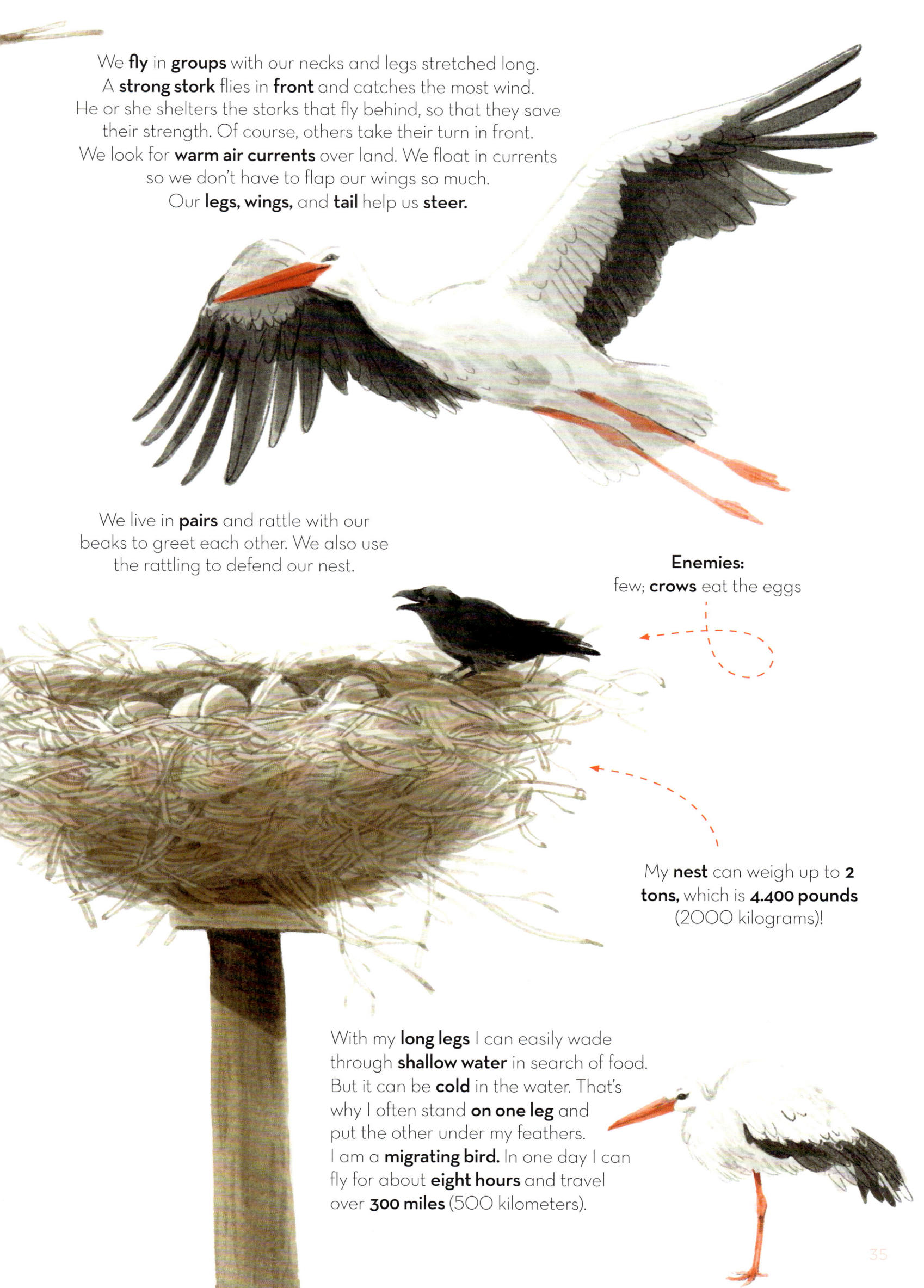

We **fly** in **groups** with our necks and legs stretched long. A **strong stork** flies in **front** and catches the most wind. He or she shelters the storks that fly behind, so that they save their strength. Of course, others take their turn in front. We look for **warm air currents** over land. We float in currents so we don't have to flap our wings so much. Our **legs, wings,** and **tail** help us **steer.**

We live in **pairs** and rattle with our beaks to greet each other. We also use the rattling to defend our nest.

Enemies:
few; **crows** eat the eggs

My **nest** can weigh up to **2 tons,** which is **4.400 pounds** (2000 kilograms)!

With my **long legs** I can easily wade through **shallow water** in search of food. But it can be **cold** in the water. That's why I often stand **on one leg** and put the other under my feathers. I am a **migrating bird.** In one day I can fly for about **eight hours** and travel over **300 miles** (500 kilometers).

Since I'm big, I need a big nest. Building it takes a lot of time. Every spring I return to my old nest. I don't want to start all over again, so I fill it up with fresh branches and grass. That's why my nest can be more than 6 feet (2 meters) high.

People think that storks bring good luck. They don't mind if we make our nest near their house.

I build my nest with dead branches and twigs that I find. At the top I lay tender plants and grass. Nice and soft to sit on!

MEERKAT

We dig so many tunnels and caves that our home looks like a maze. We take turns looking for food and standing guard. When an enemy appears, we purr, bark, or whistle as a warning. Then we run as fast as possible to a hiding place under the ground.

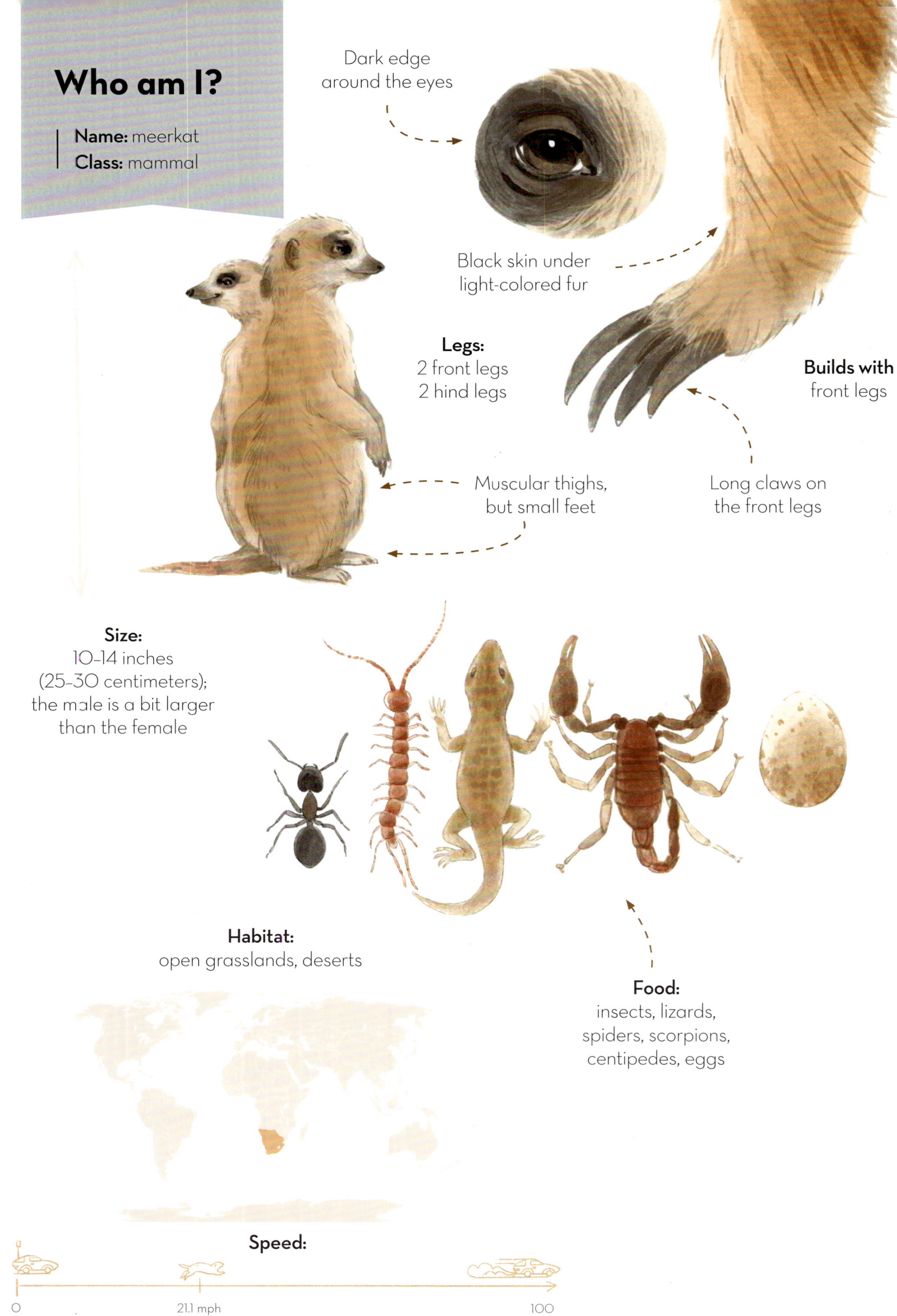

Who am I?

Name: meerkat
Class: mammal

Dark edge around the eyes

Black skin under light-colored fur

Legs:
2 front legs
2 hind legs

Builds with front legs

Muscular thighs, but small feet

Long claws on the front legs

Size:
10–14 inches (25–30 centimeters); the male is a bit larger than the female

Habitat:
open grasslands, deserts

Food:
insects, lizards, spiders, scorpions, centipedes, eggs

Speed:

0   21.1 mph   100

Enemies:

eagle   jackal   hawk   some snakes

The nights in the desert are cold. So in the morning, I stand with my **belly in the sun.** My black skin absorbs the heat quickly. I use my **tail** to keep my **balance** when I'm standing on two legs.

I'm a really **fast digger.** I like to make dust clouds to **frighten** my enemies.

The black edges around my eyes protect me from the bright sunlight. I have **great eyesight** and I keep watch for birds of prey in the sky.

Meerkats are very **social** and **live in groups** of more than **thirty animals.** We all take care of the little ones. But we can also be **aggressive** and fight with other groups.

If I'm threatened, I might **growl** or **bite** an attacker or **blow** or **spit** at it.

We live in a large network of tunnels with several entrances.
When the sun shines, we come out. When it rains or is cloudy, we often stay inside. In the afternoon we take shelter from the great heat.

You can also find dung beetles in our tunnels. They clean up our poop and lay their eggs in it. Quite a handy system to keep things neat and tidy!

We have extra shelters and tunnels near the places where we look for food. We can take shelter there if there is danger. We sometimes share the tunnels and caves with ground squirrels and yellow mongooses.

The entrances and exits are connected to all kinds of burrows by a tangle of tunnels. We live and sleep in these belowground spaces. There are nesting rooms for the little ones.

HONEYBEE

My house is a hive. It may be in a hollow tree or made of wood. We build nests with combs of wax and we fill the combs with honey, which we use for food in the winter, when there are no flowers.

Who am I?

Name: honeybee
Class: insect

Legs: 6

Builds with
legs and tongue

Size:
the smallest species measures
.12 inch (3 millimeters) and the largest
measures 1.18 inches (3 centimeters);
the worker honeybee measures
.51 inch (1.3 centimeters)

I only sting as a final resort.
If I sting something, I **lose** my
stinger and I **die.** Wasps don't
lose their stinger and can sting
often. They are more dangerous to you than I am.

A sting
with a barb

Habitat:
anywhere except where it is very cold

A long tongue
to extract nectar
from flowers

Speed:

0   14.9 mph   100

When I visit a flower, pollen sticks to my legs. Then I transfer the **pollen** to other flowers. That's how flowers make new seeds.

Food:
pollen and nectar

Enemies:
birds (such as bee-eaters and woodpeckers),

skunk

bears

There are **three types** of bees in our hive: the **queen**, the **drones**, and the **workers.** The drones are males and the workers are females. Only the workers have a stinger.

When one of the workers has found food, she performs a **dance** for the others. From the movements of the dance we learn the directions to join her there.

We are suffering from the **pesticides** that people use to spray in nature. It can kill an entire bee colony.

We don't build our whole hives by ourselves.
First we look for a space where we can live.
This is often a hollow tree or it may be a hive
that is made by people. We all crawl into it
and then I go to work with the other workers.

We change the sugar in honey into wax, and then chew the tiny pieces of wax until they become soft. Then we add the chewed wax to our honeycomb cells. We are always working hard in our hives. Yes, we are busy bees! At the end of the summer the combs are full of honey. The beekeeper comes to harvest the honey from the combs. In exchange he gives us sugar to get through the winter.

JAPANESE PUFFER FISH

I'm probably the most unusual builder in the whole world.
I build an underwater nest in the sand to attract a female.
Maybe because I don't look special myself?

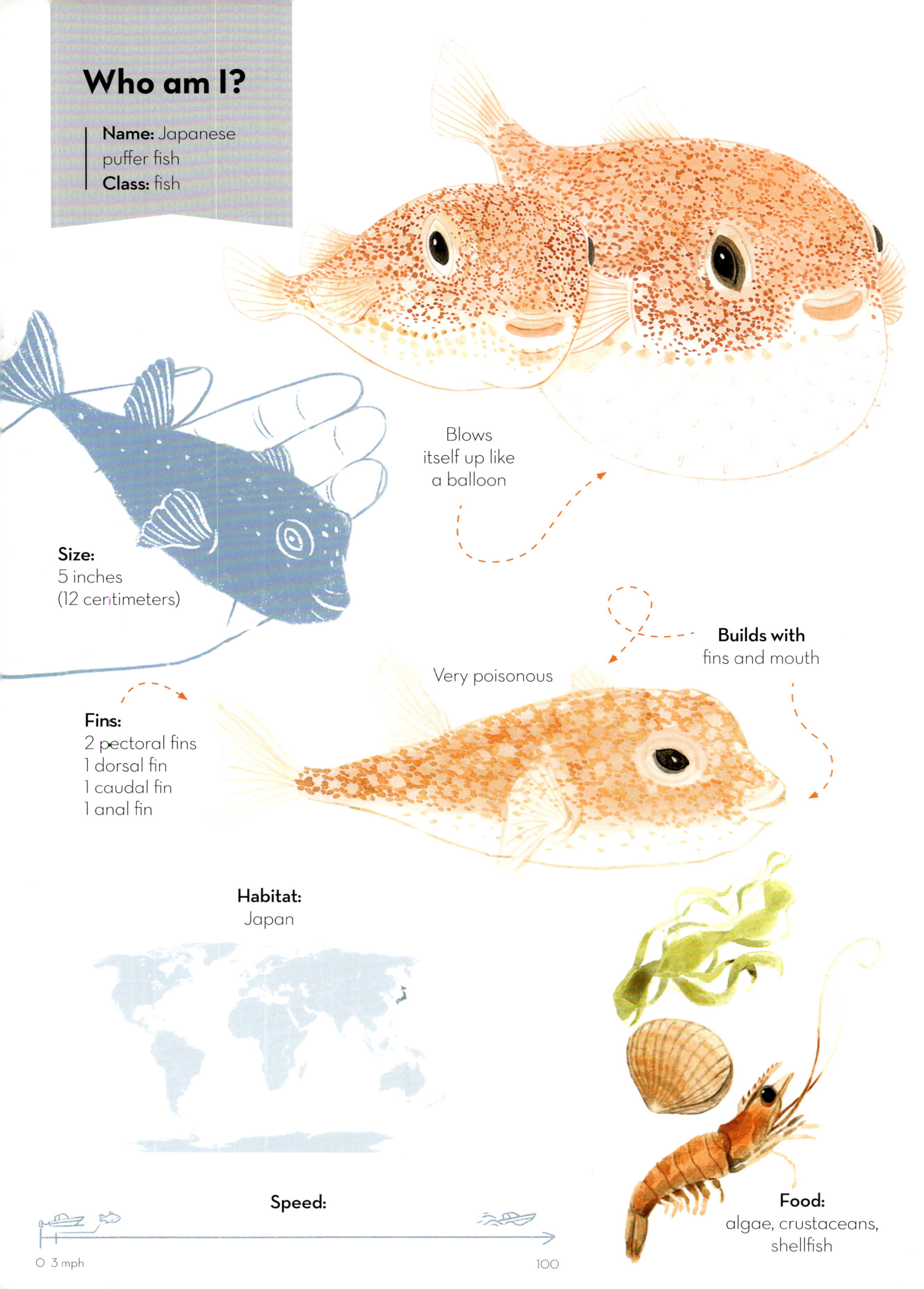

Who am I?

Name: Japanese puffer fish
Class: fish

Blows itself up like a balloon

Size:
5 inches (12 centimeters)

Very poisonous

Builds with fins and mouth

Fins:
2 pectoral fins
1 dorsal fin
1 caudal fin
1 anal fin

Habitat:
Japan

Speed:

0 3 mph

Food:
algae, crustaceans, shellfish

To scare off enemies, I'll blow myself up to be **three times bigger.** It happens very fast. Some puffer fish also have long, sharp spines that come out of their bodies, but not me.

My two **eyes** can **move separately.** So I can look at two different things at once. One eye looks for food, the other for an enemy.

I have **many enemies.** But if they eat me, they die themselves. I have enough **poison** in my body to kill an adult human being! I'm a slow swimmer, but I change direction quickly. I can even swim backwards.

Enemies: fish-eaters like sharks and dolphins

Doesn't my nest look beautiful? I build it at the bottom of the ocean. I swim back and forth and plow through the sand with my fins. I draw a circle that's about the same size as a queen-size bed. It takes more than a week to complete my nest. When a female is impressed by my artwork, she lays her eggs in the middle of the nest. When the little fish are born and they swim away, then I swim away too and make a new nest somewhere else.

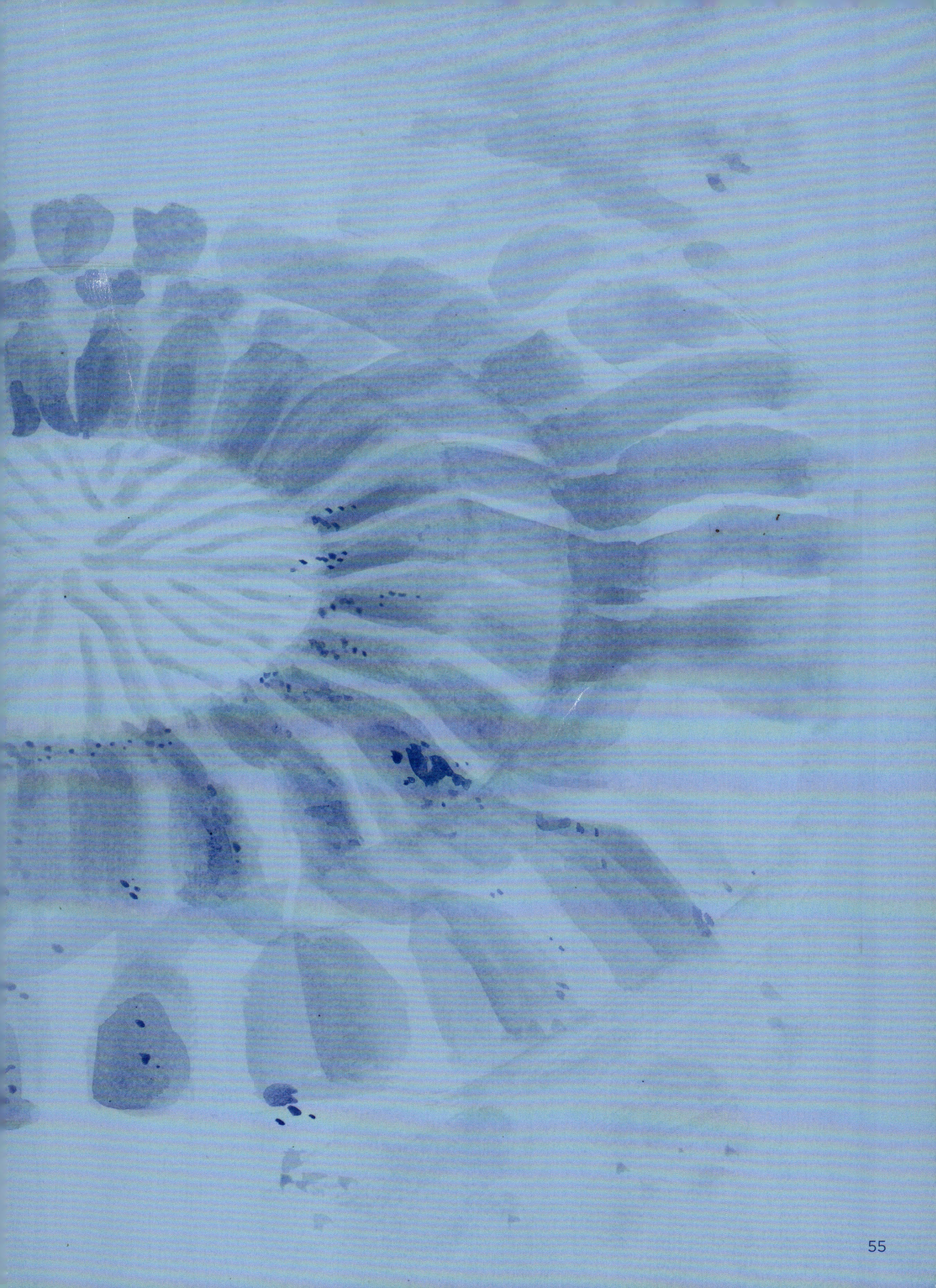

MOLE

I must be the best digger in the world. My system of tunnels is often more than 200 yards (183 meters) long. There is plenty of room to crawl around, because I live on my own—except for when I am looking for a mate.

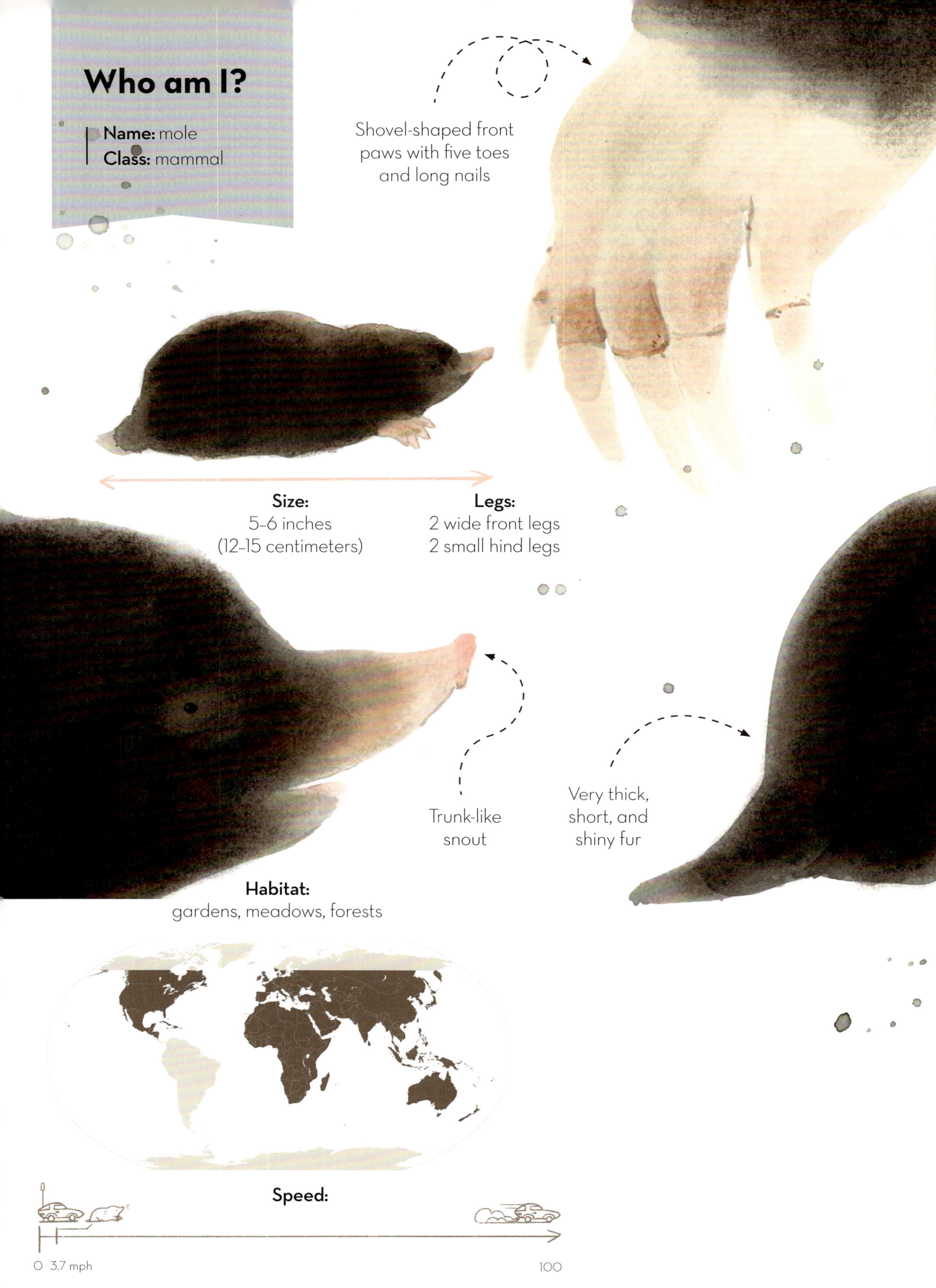

Who am I?

Name: mole
Class: mammal

Shovel-shaped front paws with five toes and long nails

Size:
5–6 inches
(12–15 centimeters)

Legs:
2 wide front legs
2 small hind legs

Trunk-like snout

Very thick, short, and shiny fur

Habitat:
gardens, meadows, forests

Speed:

O 3.7 mph

Enemies:

beavers   weasels   skunks   birds of prey   badgers   foxes

My **eyes** are **very small** which makes it hard to see. But that's okay, because I **live underground** and I don't need to see much. I can only see the difference between light and dark. I smell really well and I use vibrations to get around.

Builds with front legs

I collect hundreds of worms in my winter **storage room.** I bite off the front part of the worm. The worm stays alive, but can't move anymore. So I always have fresh food.

Food: worms and insects

I eat more than **half my weight** every **day.**

When I was born, I was completely naked and blind. And I was very small. After two weeks I had a warm coat, and after two months I was fully grown. Imagine if you grew that quickly!

With my broad front feet, I dig tunnels underground. I slide the earth behind me with a swinging movement. Every now and then I also toss the loose earth upward. This is how the molehills that you might see in a garden are created.

I dig tunnels just below the ground and like to dig in grass, because there are a lot of worms there. But I also dig down deeper. There I have a network of tunnels leading to rooms.

I dig out a bedroom, a pantry where I keep worms,
and a nesting room where the little ones are born.
After about five weeks they leave the nest and
I have my home to myself again!

We are all builders!